AUTHOR INVISIBLE

A Quick Guide to

Business Strategies

First edition

ISBN: 978-981-18-7664-6

Editing by Lord Karthikeyan Rajasaygaran

(Karls)

Contents

Foreword   iv

Preface   vii

1   Introduction to Business Strategy   1

2   Analyzing the Internal Environment   12

3   Analyzing the External Environment (PEST)   25

4   Setting Goals and Objectives   33

5   Developing a Business Model   37

6   Marketing Strategy   42

7   Sales Strategy   48

8   Financial Planning and Management   53

9   Operations Strategy   60

10 Human Resource Strategy   66

11 Risk Management   71

12 Implementation and Evaluation   80

Foreword

'A Quick Guide To Business Strategies' is well crafted with vital points on how to begin and establish a business potently highlighted.

The guidelines and advice stated, have been carefully studied and listed for readers to comprehend without effort. Each and every topic mentioned in the book is essential to everyone planning to commence a business.

All 12 headings are well supported with authentic key points suitable for the current market trend and business ventures. The guide highlights the far-sighted attitude a business owner should possess in sustaining a business and managing it effectively even in 'bear' times.

The author has clearly displayed his professional knowledge on the subject matter and thy knowledge indeed serves as an asset to anyone seeking a 'business guru'.

A simple and comprehensive book that has met its objectives productively.

Dr Ravee Vellu S
Doctor of Metaphysical Science

* * *

In wars, strategies determine the operational decisions that lead to victory and are equally applicable to businesses to succeed in their ventures. Many books on business strategies tend to leave the reader baffled which this book has rectified by providing a clear and concise guide to help the business owner take the appropriate steps to reduce the prospect of failure and increase the chance of success. The topic of analysing the internal environment provides an appropriate launch pad for business owners as they tend to focus on the external environment and neglect thorough and unabashed scrutiny of the internal dynamics of the organisation. The checklist is comprehensive enough to help the reader without overwhelming the minutiae. I am happy to note that this approach has been applied to all contents within the book and presented in a highly readable and engaging manner.

M Thiyagarajan
B.A, B.Soc Sci (Hons), M.A. Area Studies (Southeast Asia)

* * *

Karthikeyan has authored an interesting book for entrepreneurs, business students and business owners. It is a pocket guide for anyone who wants to understand key terms and tenets in business and the associated strategies. I have known Karls Karthikeyan for over 15 years. Karls Karthikeyan's straight-to-the-face approach to life is closely reflected in his book. The points are conveyed objectively with no extra descriptives or floral language.

The striking feature of the book to me was the organization of the ideas. Without proper vision and clarity of thought, such an organization will not be possible. It is highly textual and academic yet simple and effective.

While the former will entice business students and academics alike, the latter makes it easily palatable for non-academics looking to obtain a quick understanding of the aspects of business. The language is devoid of jargon, high-sounding words and complicated sentences making it easy for everyone to understand the author.

The good thing about this book is that you can open any page or any section and start reading it. Some books are written linearly while some texts are nonlinear. While Karls Karthikeyan has adopted this approach of linear text with the chapters ordered and organized chronologically for business personnel, you can still read from any chapter, and it will be a meaningful standalone text. Every time you read any section; it gives a new perspective of things.

You can also see his cheeky side in certain instances. He quotes Gandhi to explain the significance of customers and he quotes himself on how spraying perfumes cannot mask the odour of a dead rat.

I wish Karls Karthikeyan and the book to do very well and look forward to reading more of his works in more genres and topics.

Elavazhagan Murugan MS PhD
Founder and Director
PrEl's Technologies Private Limited, Singapore PrEl's
Biotech India Private Limited, India

Preface

The Quick Guide series is for everyone who has little time on their hands and wants a quick reference or guide. Our first series starts off with Business Strategy basics mainly for people who have been wanting to start a business or Business professionals who are looking back to their basics to refresh their memories. This is the first book in the series written by a passionate learning individual who wants to share his knowledge with the world.

The Business Strategy Guide is a quick guide designed to help business owners and managers develop and implement a successful business strategy. The guide covers a wide range of topics, including the importance of developing a mission statement and values, conducting a market analysis, setting goals and objectives, creating a business model, developing a marketing strategy, and implementing a sales strategy.

The guide provides in-depth information on each topic, examples, and practical tips for success. It emphasizes the importance of taking a strate- gic approach to business planning and provides tools and techniques for creating a comprehensive and effective business strategy.

Throughout the guide, there is a strong focus on the importance of understanding the target customer and creating strategies that align with their needs and preferences. The guide also stresses the importance of ongoing evaluation and adaptation, highlighting the need for businesses to continuously monitor and adjust their strategies to ensure long-term success.

The best way to use the strategies in this guide is not to read through but rather to read each chapter and reflect on their current business models before moving on to the next chapter. The book will provide different interpretations at different stages of the business person, thus it will be an ever-green book that will reside on your shelf for ages to come.

Overall, the Business Strategy Guide provides a valuable resource for business owners and managers looking to develop and implement a successful business strategy. Its practical advice and comprehensive coverage of key topics make it an essential resource for anyone looking to take their business to the next level.

1

Introduction to Business Strategy

A business strategy is a long-term plan of action designed to achieve specific goals or objectives for a business. It is a comprehensive plan that outlines the way a company intends to compete in the market, differentiate itself from competitors, and create value for its customers and stakeholders.

A business strategy typically involves several elements, such as a company's vision and mission, analysis of the market and competition, identification of target customers and their needs, identification of key strengths and weaknesses, and development of a plan to achieve the desired outcomes. This plan may include specific tactics and initiatives, such as product development, marketing campaigns, partnerships and collaborations, cost-cutting measures, and resource allocation.

The ultimate goal of a business strategy is to create a sustainable competitive advantage that allows a company to succeed and grow over the long term. This involves making choices about which markets to compete in, how to differentiate products or services from competitors, and how to allocate resources effectively to achieve the desired outcomes.

Business strategy is a plan or set of actions that a company develops to achieve its long-term goals and objectives. It involves making decisions on how to allocate resources, develop and market products or services, enter new markets, and compete with rivals. A well-defined business strategy is critical for a company's success, as it guides the organization's activities towards a common goal and helps it to stay ahead of the competition. The strategy should take into account factors such as market trends, customer needs, technological advancements, regulatory requirements, and financial considerations, among others. It should also be regularly reviewed and adapted to ensure that it remains relevant and effective in achieving the company's objectives.

Importance of Business Strategy: Having a solid business strategy is critical for any organization. A well-defined strategy can help companies to differentiate themselves from competitors, identify new opportunities and potential markets, build a sustainable business model, make informed business decisions, and achieve long-term growth and success.

1. Helps achieve business goals: A well-defined business strategy sets clear goals and objectives for the organization, which allows the organization to focus on what's essential and allocate resources accordingly. This ensures that the company is moving in the right direction and that all efforts are aligned with its overall vision and mission.

2. Guided decision-making: Business strategy provides a framework for making important business decisions, such as choosing which markets to enter, which products to offer, and how to allocate resources. A clear business strategy helps managers make informed decisions that are consistent with the company's overall goals and

objectives.

3. Enhances competitive advantage: A strong business strategy can help a company differentiate itself from its competitors and gain a competitive advantage. By identifying the company's unique strengths and weaknesses, a business strategy can help the company position itself in the market and develop a sustainable competitive advantage.

4. Facilitates resource allocation: A business strategy helps managers allocate resources effectively by identifying the areas of the busi- ness that are most important to achieving the company's goals. This ensures that resources are used efficiently and effectively and that the company is investing in the right areas.

5. Improves performance: A well-executed business strategy can lead to improved performance and financial results. By setting clear goals and objectives, and aligning resources and efforts towards achieving them, a business strategy can help a company improve its bottom line and achieve long-term success.

Components of Business Strategy: Business strategy comprises several key components, including vision, mission, goals and objectives, market analysis, Market analysis, business model, marketing strategy, sales strategy, financial planning and management, operations strategy, human resource strategy, and risk management.

Vision:

A company vision is a statement that describes the company's long-term aspirations and goals. It is a forward-looking statement that defines what the company wants to achieve in the future and provides a sense of direction and purpose for the organization.

A company vision typically includes a description of the company's core values, its strategic objectives, and the impact it hopes to have on the world. It should be a concise and memorable statement that inspires and motivates employees, stakeholders, and customers alike.

A well-crafted company vision can help align the organization around a common goal, and provide a sense of purpose and direction. It can also serve as a guide for decision-making, as it provides a clear framework for evaluating opportunities and assessing whether they align with the company's long-term objectives. Overall, a strong company vision is an important component of a successful business strategy.

Mission:

A company mission is a statement that describes the purpose and reason for a company's existence. It defines the company's core values, the markets it serves, and the products or services it offers.

A company mission statement typically includes a description of the company's target customers, its unique selling proposition, and the impact it hopes to have on society. It should be a clear and concise statement that communicates the company's purpose and values to employees, customers, and stakeholders.

A well-crafted company mission statement can help guide decision-making and ensure that all activities within the organization are aligned with its core values and purpose. It can also serve as a powerful marketing tool, as it communicates the company's unique selling proposition and value proposition to customers.

Overall, a strong company mission is an important component of a successful business strategy, as it helps define the company's purpose and values and provides a clear direction for the organization.

Goals and Objectives:

Goals and objectives are two related but distinct concepts that are commonly used in business and organizational settings to help guide planning, decision-making, and performance management.

Goals are broad, high-level statements that describe what an organization wants to achieve over a long-term period, such as several years or more. They are typically qualitative and aspirational in nature and often represent the organization's overarching strategic direction. Examples of goals might include increasing market share, improving customer satisfaction, or expanding into new markets.

Objectives, on the other hand, are more specific and measurable statements that describe what an organization wants to achieve over a shorter time frame, such as a year or less. They are typically more concrete and focused than goals and are designed to support the achievement of broader strategic goals. Examples of objectives might include increasing sales by a certain percentage, reducing production costs, or improving employee retention rates.

Market Analysis:

Market analysis is the process of evaluating the current and future potential of a particular market, industry or product. It involves gathering and analyzing data about a market's size, trends, competition, customers, and other factors that can influence the demand and supply of goods or services.

Market analysis helps businesses to identify opportunities, assess risks, and make informed decisions about their marketing and sales strategies. It is an essential tool for companies to understand their customers and competitors, as well as to identify the factors that affect their business.

The process of market analysis typically includes gathering data from primary and secondary sources, analyzing the data to identify trends and patterns, and using this information to make informed decisions about market entry, pricing, product development, and other important business decisions. The results of market analysis can be used to create a comprehensive marketing plan that aligns with the needs and preferences of the target market.

Business Model:

A business model is a framework that outlines how a company creates, delivers, and captures value. It describes the way a business generates revenue, manages costs, and makes a profit. A business model typically includes a description of the company's target customers, the products or services it offers, the channels through which it reaches customers, the resources it needs to operate, and the activities it engages in to deliver value to customers.

In essence, a business model is a plan for how a company will make money and sustain itself over time. Different types of businesses may have different business models, depending on factors such as the industry, the target market, and the competitive landscape. Some common examples of business models include subscription-based models, premium models, and advertising-based models.

Marketing Strategy:

Marketing strategy is the overall plan that a company uses to promote its products or services to its target audience. It involves identifying the company's target market, understanding the needs and preferences of that market, and creating a plan to effectively reach and persuade those customers to purchase the company's products or services.

A marketing strategy may include various components such as market research, product development, pricing strategies, distribution channels, and promotion tactics. The strategy must be designed to align with the company's overall business goals and objectives and should be flexible enough to adapt to changing market conditions and customer needs.

Ultimately, the goal of a marketing strategy is to increase sales and profits by building brand awareness, establishing customer loyalty, and creating a competitive advantage in the marketplace.

Sales Strategy:

A sales strategy is a plan of action that outlines how a company will sell its products or services to potential customers. It includes a set of tactics and approaches designed to help a business achieve its sales goals and objectives. The sales strategy typically involves identifying target customers, developing a value proposition that resonates with them, and determining the best channels and methods to reach and engage with those customers.

A well-defined sales strategy will usually include the following components:

1. Sales goals and objectives: This outlines what the business hopes to achieve through its sales efforts, such as revenue targets, market share goals, and customer acquisition targets.
2. Target customers: This involves identifying the types of customers who are most likely to purchase the business's products or services and understanding their needs, preferences, and pain points.
3. Value proposition: This describes how the business's products or services provide value to customers and how they differentiate from competitors.
4. Sales channels: This outlines the various channels through which the business will sell its products or services, such as direct sales,

online sales, or through partners and resellers.

5. Sales tactics: This involves determining the specific actions and tactics that the business will use to sell its products or services, such as pricing, promotions, advertising, and sales presentations.

6. Sales team and resources: This involves identifying the resources and personnel required to execute the sales strategy effectively, including the sales team, marketing resources, and technology platforms.

A successful sales strategy aligns sales activities with the overall business strategy and helps ensure that the business can meet its revenue and growth objectives.

Financial Planning and Management:

Financial planning and management for business refer to the process of creating a financial plan and managing the financial resources of a company to achieve its goals and objectives. This involves forecasting future financial needs, developing a budget, monitoring financial performance, and making strategic financial decisions to optimize profitability and growth.

Financial planning is the process of identifying the company's financial goals, determining the financial resources required to achieve those goals, and creating a plan to allocate those resources effectively. This includes forecasting revenue, expenses, and cash flow, as well as identifying potential risks and opportunities.

Financial management involves implementing the financial plan and managing the company's financial resources on an ongoing basis. This includes monitoring financial performance, making financial decisions based on data and analysis, managing cash flow, and ensuring compliance with financial regulations.

Effective financial planning and management are crucial for the success of any business, as they provide a clear understanding of the company's financial position, enable informed decision-making, and help to ensure financial stability and long-term sustainability.

Operations Strategy:

Operations strategy in business is the set of decisions and actions that a company undertakes to design and manage its operations in order to achieve its overall business objectives. It involves developing a plan for how a company will utilize its resources, such as people, technology, and physical assets, to produce and deliver its products or services efficiently and effectively.

The operations strategy encompasses a range of activities such as supply chain management, process design, capacity planning, quality management, and innovation. It also involves the integration of various functions within the company, including marketing, finance, and human resources, to ensure that the operations are aligned with the overall business strategy.

The goal of operations strategy is to create a competitive advantage for the company by differentiating its operations from those of its competi- tors. This can be achieved through various means, such as developing unique production processes, optimizing supply chain management, or investing in innovative technologies.

Overall, the operations strategy plays a critical role in the success of a business by ensuring that its operations are efficient, effective, and aligned with the overall business objectives.

Human Resource Strategy:

Human Resource Strategy (HR Strategy) refers to the overall plan or approach that an organization adopts to manage its workforce in order to achieve its business goals and objectives. It involves aligning the organization's human resources policies and practices with its overall business strategy to maximize employee performance, productivity, and satisfaction.

An effective HR strategy takes into account factors such as the organization's culture, values, and mission, as well as the current and future needs of the workforce. It also includes strategies for attracting, recruiting, developing, and retaining employees, as well as for managing performance, providing rewards and recognition, and promoting diversity, equity, and inclusion.

Ultimately, an HR strategy should enable an organization to build a skilled, motivated, and engaged workforce that is aligned with its business goals, and that can adapt to changing circumstances and market conditions.

Risk Management:

Risk management is the process of identifying, assessing, and controlling risks that may impact an organization's operations, assets, or objectives. It involves developing strategies and procedures to minimize the negative effects of potential risks, while also maximizing the opportunities that may arise from managing those risks effectively.

Risk management typically involves several steps, including:

1. Risk identification: Identifying potential risks that could impact the organization.
2. Risk assessment: Evaluating the likelihood and potential impact of each identified risk.
3. Risk mitigation: Developing strategies and procedures to minimize or eliminate the risks.
4. Risk monitoring and review: Continuously monitoring and review-

ing risks to ensure that the risk management strategies are effective and up-to-date.

Effective risk management can help organizations to avoid or minimize potential losses and liabilities, improve decision-making, and achieve their objectives in a more secure and sustainable way. This is where SWOT and PEST analysis are majorly used in organizations.

In conclusion, developing a successful business strategy is critical for achieving long-term success. By defining the company's vision, mission, goals and objectives, conducting market and Market analyses, developing a business model, marketing and sales strategies, financial planning and management, operations and human resource strategies, and implementing risk management, businesses can create a strong model that paves the way to success.

2

Analyzing the Internal Environment

To develop a successful business strategy, it is essential to analyze the internal environment of the organization. The internal environment consists of the company's resources, capabilities, and core competencies, as well as its organizational structure and culture. In this chapter, we will explore the key elements of the internal environment and how they can impact the development of a successful business strategy.

* * *

Resources

Resources refer to the assets that a company has at its disposal, such as financial resources, physical resources, and human resources. To analyze the internal environment, it is important to identify the company's resources and evaluate its strengths and weaknesses.

Financial Resources

Financial resources include the company's financial assets, such as cash reserves, investments, and credit lines. It is important to assess the company's financial resources to determine its ability to invest in new projects, products, or services, and to weather economic downturns. A company's financial resources refer to the various sources of funding and capital that it uses to finance its operations and investments. These resources include both internal and external sources of funds, such as:

1. Equity: This refers to the ownership stake that investors have in the company, which is typically represented by the common or preferred stock. Equity financing allows companies to raise capital without taking on debt, and also provides investors with a share of the company's profits.

2. Debt: This includes any loans or bonds that a company takes on to finance its operations or investments. Debt financing typically involves paying interest on the loan or bond and may require the company to provide collateral to secure the loan.

3. Retained earnings: These are profits that the company has earned and reinvested back into the business, rather than paying out as dividends to shareholders. Retained earnings are an important source of internal financing for companies, as they allow them to fund new projects or investments without taking on additional debt or diluting shareholder ownership.

4. Operating cash flow: This refers to the cash generated by a company's day-to-day operations, such as sales and expenses. Operating cash flow is an important measure of a company's financial health, as it indicates whether the company is generating enough cash to cover its costs and invest in future growth.

5. Asset sales: Companies may also generate cash by selling assets that they no longer need or want, such as real estate, equipment, or intellectual property.

Managing a company's financial resources effectively is critical to its success, as it enables the company to finance its operations and invest in future growth while also maintaining a healthy balance sheet and cash flow.

Physical Resources

Physical resources include the company's tangible assets, such as equipment, facilities, and inventory. It is important to assess the company's physical resources to determine its capacity to meet customer demand and to identify any bottlenecks or inefficiencies in the production process. These resources can include the following but are not limited to:

1. Land and buildings: This includes the company's office space, manufacturing facilities, and any other physical properties that it owns or leases.
2. Equipment and machinery: This includes any tools, machinery, or other equipment that the company uses in its operations, such as computers, vehicles, or manufacturing equipment.
3. Inventory: This includes any goods or materials that the company has in stock, whether raw materials or finished products.
4. Infrastructure: This includes the physical infrastructure that supports the company's operations, such as roads, bridges, and utility networks.
5. Intellectual property: This includes any patents, trademarks, or other intellectual property that the company owns, as well as any proprietary technology or processes that it uses in its operations.

Effective management of a company's physical resources is important for several reasons. First, it ensures that the company has the tools and resources necessary to conduct its operations effectively and efficiently. Second, it helps to protect the company's assets and minimize the risk of loss or damage. Finally, it can help the company to identify opportunities for growth and expansion, by identifying areas where it can invest in new equipment, facilities, or technologies to improve its operations and stay competitive in the marketplace. Do take note that many of these resources are interrelated and would not make any sense to see them as separate resources, thus the link or permanent or temporary relations towards the resources have to be taken into consideration.

Human Resources

Human resources refer to the company's workforce, including its employees, managers, and executives. It is important to assess the company's human resources to determine the expertise, experience, and skill set of its employees, and to identify any gaps that need to be addressed through training or hiring. Human resources on the terminology itself might be undermining the importance of these resources. No matter how much machinery, automation or Artificial Intelligence is created there is no replacement for a human in the organizational setting. It is the far most important and difficult resource to handle. With changing times so does the expectation of the employee and understanding the needs and wants of your employee to chart a long-term plan makes most companies successful or vice versa.

The role of human resources and the sectors to pay attention to are as follows as this would set the foundation of a new aspiring member entering into YOUR organization:

1. Recruitment: HR departments are responsible for recruiting and hiring new employees, which involves advertising job openings, screening resumes and applications, and conducting interviews to find the best candidates for the job.

2. Training and development: Once employees are hired, HR is responsible for ensuring that they are trained and supported in their roles, which can include providing orientation and on boarding, offering ongoing training and development programs, and providing coaching and mentoring to help employees achieve their goals. This can be far more elaborate in terms of Skills Training and Critical Core skills development.

3. Performance management: HR departments are responsible for managing employee performance and ensuring that employees are meeting their goals and objectives. This can include conducting performance reviews, providing feedback and support, and developing performance improvement plans when necessary.

4. Compensation and benefits: HR departments are responsible for managing employee compensation and benefits, which can include setting salaries and wages, administering employee benefits programs, and managing payroll.

5. Employee relations: HR departments are responsible for managing employee relations and ensuring that employees are treated fairly and respectfully. This can include addressing employee grievances, managing workplace conflicts, and ensuring that the company's policies and procedures are followed consistently and fairly.

Effective management of human resources is critical to a company's success, as it ensures that the company has the right people in the right roles, that those people are supported and developed, and that the company's culture and values are reflected in its workforce. It also helps to ensure that the company is complying with all relevant laws and regulations related to employment and labour.

Capabilities and Core Competencies

Capabilities and core competencies refer to the company's unique strengths and abilities. To analyze the internal environment, it is important to identify the company's capabilities and core competencies and evaluate its strengths and weaknesses.

Capabilities

Capabilities refer to the company's ability to perform specific tasks or functions. For example, a company may have the capability to design and manufacture high-quality products or to provide exceptional customer service. It is important to assess the company's capabilities to determine its competitive advantage and to identify any areas that need improve- ment. The capabilities of a company refer to its ability to perform certain tasks or activities effectively, efficiently, and consistently.

Some common capabilities of a company might include:

1. Manufacturing: The ability to design and produce high-quality products in large quantities, often through the use of specialized equipment and manufacturing processes.
2. Marketing and sales: The ability to create and execute effective marketing strategies, build strong relationships with customers, and drive sales growth.
3. Research and development: The ability to conduct research and development activities to create new products, improve existing products, or develop new technologies.
4. Logistics and supply chain management: The ability to manage the flow of goods and services from suppliers to customers, including transportation, warehousing, and distribution.
5. Customer service: The ability to provide high-quality customer service, including responding to inquiries, addressing complaints, and resolving issues in a timely and effective manner.

To develop and maintain these capabilities, companies often invest in training and development programs, technology and equipment upgrades, and process improvements. They may also partner with other companies, acquire new businesses or technologies, or engage in other strategic activities to strengthen their capabilities and stay competitive in the marketplace.

Regardless of the person, every position should have standard operat- ing procedures along with roles and responsibilities, this is so that a key performance index can be given to all staff and management to ensure the company culture and expectations are clearly defined.

Ultimately, a company's capabilities are a key factor in its ability to succeed in its chosen markets and achieve its strategic objectives. By building and maintaining strong capabilities, companies can differenti- ate themselves from their competitors, attract and retain customers, and drive long-term growth and profitability. A company's unique selling point does not necessarily have to be a product it can be company culture, service speed etc.

Core Competencies

A company's core competency refers to the unique strengths or abilities that set it apart from its competitors and enables it to create value for its customers. These competencies can be based on a wide range of factors, including the company's products or services, its technology or intellectual property, its distribution or supply chain, its customer service, or its culture and values.

Some key characteristics of a company's core competencies might include:

1. Uniqueness: Core competencies are often based on unique strengths or resources that are difficult for competitors to replicate or imitate.

2. Value creation: Core competencies should enable the company to create significant value for its customers, such as by improving product quality, reducing costs, or enhancing the customer experience.

3. Strategic fit: Core competencies should be aligned with the company's overall strategic objectives and goals, helping to support its growth and success over the long term.

4. Sustainability: Core competencies should be sustainable over time, meaning that they can continue to provide value and competitive advantage even as market conditions and technologies evolve. in the current time Worker from home has become widely revived thanks to the pandemic, companies have started to realise that the need for a physical office might not be necessary and hence allow more funds to be distributed to other areas of business such as staff development, business continuity plans, cloud services etc.

Some examples of companies with strong core competencies might include:

1. Apple: Apple's core competency is its ability to design and develop innovative, user-friendly products that are highly desirable to consumers.

2. Amazon: Amazon's core competency is its vast, highly efficient supply chain and distribution network, which enables it to offer a wide range of products at competitive prices with fast delivery.

3. Google: Google's core competency is its advanced search algorithms and data analytics capabilities, which enable it to provide highly relevant search results and personalized content to users.

By leveraging their core competencies, companies can differentiate themselves from their competitors, attract and retain customers, and drive long-term growth and profitability. However, it is important for companies to regularly evaluate and evolve their core competencies to stay competitive and relevant in a rapidly changing marketplace.

Organizational Structure

Organizational structure refers to how a company is organized, including its hierarchy, departments, and reporting lines. Organizational structure plays a crucial role in a company's strategy as it determines how work is organized and decision-making processes are structured within the organization. An effective organizational structure can help a company to achieve its strategic goals by providing a clear framework for the allocation of resources, the management of key business processes, and the alignment of individual and team goals with the overall objectives of the company.

Some important ways in which organizational structure can impact a company's strategy include:

1. Resource allocation: The structure of a company determines how resources such as people, capital, and technology are allocated across different departments and functions. An effective organizational structure can ensure that resources are used efficiently and effectively, enabling the company to achieve its strategic goals.

2. Decision-making: The organizational structure of a company also influences how decisions are made, by whom, and at what level. An effective structure can facilitate decision-making that is aligned with the company's strategy, enabling faster and more effective implementation of strategic initiatives.

3. Communication and collaboration: The structure of a company can also impact communication and collaboration among different teams and departments. A well-designed structure can encourage open communication, knowledge sharing, and collaboration, which

are critical for implementing a successful strategy.

4. Agility and adaptability: Organizational structure can impact a company's ability to respond quickly to changes in the marketplace or to adjust its strategy in response to new opportunities or challenges. A flexible and adaptable structure can enable a company to be more responsive and agile in a rapidly changing environment.

In summary, the organizational structure is a key factor in a company's ability to execute its strategy effectively. By aligning structure with strategy, companies can ensure that they have the right resources, decision-making processes, communication channels, and agility to succeed in a competitive marketplace.

Culture

Culture refers to the shared values, beliefs, and practices of an organization. It is important to assess the company's culture to determine its impact on employee behavior and performance and to identify any areas that need to be addressed to align the company's culture with its goals and objectives.

There are some of the key reasons why business culture is important:

1. Employee engagement and retention: A positive business culture can help to attract and retain top talent by creating a sense of purpose, belonging, and fulfillment among employees. When employees feel engaged and connected to the company's values and mission, they are more likely to be motivated, productive, and committed to the organization.

2. Innovation and creativity: A strong business culture can encourage innovation and creativity by creating an environment where employees feel empowered to share ideas, take risks, and challenge the

status quo. By fostering a culture of experimentation and learning, companies can stay ahead of the curve and remain competitive in a rapidly changing marketplace.

3. Customer satisfaction: Business culture can also impact customer satisfaction by influencing the attitudes and behaviors of employees toward customers. A culture that prioritizes customer service, for example, can help to create loyal customers who are more likely to recommend the company to others.

4. Brand reputation: A company's culture can also impact its brand reputation by shaping the perceptions of customers, employees, and other stakeholders. A positive culture can help to build trust, credibility, and goodwill among stakeholders, while a negative culture can damage the company's reputation and undermine its success.

In summary, business culture is an important driver of employee engagement, innovation, customer satisfaction, and brand reputation. By creating a strong, positive culture, companies can attract and retain top talent, drive innovation and growth, and build a strong foundation for long-term success.

Conclusion

Analyzing the internal environment is an essential step in the development of a successful business strategy. By evaluating the company's resources, capabilities, core competencies, organizational structure and culture, companies can identify their strengths and weaknesses to develop strategies that capitalize on their strengths and mitigate their weaknesses. This information can be used to develop a road map for success that considers the company's unique strengths and abilities, as well as the challenges and opportunities within the business environment.

In addition to the key elements discussed in the chapter, there are several other factors to consider when analyzing the internal environment of an organization.

One of these factors is the company's history and past performance. By examining the company's past performance, including financial results, customer satisfaction, and employee turnover, companies can identify trends and patterns that can inform their future strategy. This information can help identify areas where the company has been successful in the past, as well as areas where improvements can be made.

Another factor to consider is the company's intellectual property. Intellectual property refers to the company's patents, trademarks, copyrights, and other intangible assets. These assets can be a key source of competitive advantage, and it is important to evaluate the company's intellectual property and ensure that it is protected and properly utilized.

In addition, it is important to consider the company's stakeholder relationships. Stakeholders include employees, customers, suppliers, investors, and other parties that have an interest in the company's success. By analyzing these relationships, companies can identify potential areas of conflict or opportunity and develop strategies to manage these relationships in a way that supports the company's overall goals and objectives.

Finally, it is important to consider the company's level of innovation and adaptability. In today's rapidly changing business environment, companies that can innovate and adapt to changing market conditions are more likely to succeed. By evaluating the company's level of innovation and adaptability, companies can identify areas where improvements can be made and develop strategies to foster a culture of innovation and adaptability within the organization.

By taking these factors into account, companies can develop a more comprehensive understanding of their internal environment and make more informed decisions when developing their business strategy. This, in turn, can help them capitalize on their strengths, mitigate their weaknesses, and achieve their goals and objectives.

3

Analyzing the External Environment (PEST)

When developing a business strategy, companies must consider not only their internal strengths and weaknesses but also the external factors that can impact their success. These external factors are collectively referred to as the external environment and can be divided into several categories, including economic, political, social, technological and competitive factors in short PEST-Com. By analyzing the external environment, companies can gain insights into potential opportunities and threats that may impact their business, allowing them to develop a strategy that takes into account these external factors.

1. Economic Factors

Economic factors refer to the state of the economy and its impact on consumer behavior and demand for products or services. Companies must consider economic factors such as interest rates, inflation, and unemployment when developing their business strategy. During periods of economic recession, consumers may be more price-sensitive and less likely to spend money on non-essential items, which could impact a company's sales and profitability. On the other hand, during periods of economic growth, consumers may be more willing to spend money, creating potential opportunities for companies.

When analyzing the economic factors of the external environment, companies should consider not only the state of the overall economy but also the economic conditions specific to their industry and target market. For example, a luxury goods retailer may be less impacted by a recession than a discount retailer because their target customers may be less price-sensitive. Companies should also consider global economic conditions and their impact on their business, as well as any potential currency fluctuations that may impact their profitability.

- Inflation is the rate at which the general price level of goods and services is increasing over time. High inflation rates can lead to increased costs for businesses, as they must pay more for materials, labor, and other expenses. This can lead to a decrease in profits and competitiveness.

- Interest rates impact the cost of borrowing for businesses. When interest rates are high, it becomes more expensive for businesses to borrow money, which can reduce investment and growth. Conversely, when interest rates are low, businesses may be more likely to borrow money for investment and expansion.

- Exchange rates refer to the value of one currency relative to another. For businesses that engage in international trade, exchange rates can have a significant impact on profitability. A strong domestic currency can make exports more expensive and reduce competitiveness, while a weak currency can make imports more expensive and increase costs.

- The overall level of economic activity in a country can impact the success of businesses. When the economy is growing, businesses may experience increased demand for their products and services, which can lead to increased sales and profits. Conversely, during a recession or economic downturn, businesses may struggle to maintain sales and profitability.

2. Political Factors

Political factors refer to government regulations and policies that can impact a company's business. Companies must consider the regulatory environment in which they operate, as well as any potential changes to laws or policies that could impact their business. For example, new environmental regulations could increase a company's costs and impact its profitability, while changes to tax policy could impact a company's bottom line.

- Regulatory environment: Government policies and regulations can affect businesses by creating rules that must be followed or by providing incentives or disincentives for certain behaviors. For example, environmental regulations can require businesses to reduce their carbon footprint, which can increase costs, or tax incentives can encourage businesses to invest in research and development.

- Trade policies: Government policies related to trade can impact businesses that import or export goods. Changes in tariffs or trade agreements can affect the cost of goods, which can impact profitability and competitiveness.

- Political stability: Political instability, such as coups, civil wars, or other forms of unrest, can disrupt business operations and affect the economy. For example, supply chains may be disrupted, investments may be postponed, and consumer confidence may decline.

- Taxation: Government taxation policies can impact businesses by increasing or decreasing the cost of doing business. Higher taxes can decrease profitability, while tax incentives can encourage investment and growth.

- Labor laws: Government policies related to labor laws can impact businesses by regulating wages, benefits, and working conditions. Changes in labor laws can affect the cost of labor and employee morale, which can impact productivity and profitability.

Politics can have a significant impact on businesses. Business leaders need to stay informed about government policies and regulations and be prepared to adapt to changing political environments in order to maintain profitability and competitiveness. In addition to regulations and policies, companies must also consider the political stability of the countries in which they operate. Political instability can lead to a range of issues, including supply chain disruptions, changes in labour laws, and increased security risks. Companies should also consider the impact of geopolitical events, such as trade wars or global pandemics, on their business. Many companies dont give enough importance to the political aspect of where they are operating mostly due to familiarity but with the ability to setup company anywhere in the world digitally the aspect of having a company in a country that you do not reside in might proof beneficial at times.

3. Social Factors

Social factors refer to demographic trends and cultural norms that can impact a company's success. Companies must consider the changing needs and preferences of their target customers, as well as broader societal trends that could impact their business. When analyzing social factors, companies should consider not only the changing needs and preferences of their target customers but also broader societal trends that may impact their industry.

- Demographics, such as age, gender, income, and education level, can impact consumer preferences and behavior. For example, a business selling luxury products may target affluent consumers, while a business selling budget products may target lower-income consumers.

- Cultural norms and values can also influence consumer behavior. For example, businesses may need to consider different cultural attitudes towards advertising, product packaging, and customer service in different markets.

- Social trends, such as changing attitudes towards health and wellness or environmental sustainability, can influence consumer preferences and behavior. Businesses that are able to respond to these trends by offering products and services that meet these needs may have a competitive advantage.

- Consumer attitudes towards businesses and brands can impact customer loyalty and purchasing behavior. For example, businesses that are perceived as socially responsible may be more attractive to consumers who value sustainability and ethical practices.

Social factors can have a significant impact on businesses by influencing consumer behavior, shaping market trends, and creating opportunities for businesses to innovate and differentiate themselves. Understanding these factors and responding to changing social trends is essential for businesses that want to remain competitive and grow over the long term.

4. Technological Factors

Technological factors refer to advances in technology that can impact a company's business. Companies must consider the impact of new technologies on their industry, as well as their ability to adopt and leverage new technologies to improve their operations and stay compet- itive. Technological advancements can create both opportunities and threats for businesses. Companies must stay up-to-date with the latest technological developments and understand how these developments may impact their industry. For example, advancements in artificial intelligence may allow companies to automate certain tasks and improve efficiency, while also creating potential job losses. Companies must also consider the potential risks associated with new technologies, such as data breaches or cyber attacks.

Technology has revolutionized the way businesses operate, communicate, and interact with customers, suppliers, and other stakeholders. Therefore, businesses must stay abreast of technological developments to remain relevant and competitive in the marketplace.

Some of the technological factors that businesses should consider include:

- Automation: Technology has made it possible for businesses to automate many of their processes, resulting in increased efficiency, reduced costs, and improved accuracy.
- Digitalization: The digitalization of business processes and operations has made it easier for businesses to reach customers, access

new markets, and increase revenue.

- Connectivity: Advances in technology have made it possible for businesses to communicate and collaborate with stakeholders across the globe, increasing their reach and scope.
- Cybersecurity: With the increase in digitalization, cybersecurity threats have also become more prevalent, and businesses must take steps to protect themselves and their customers from cyber attacks.
- Innovation: Technology continues to evolve at a rapid pace, and businesses that are able to innovate and stay ahead of the curve will have a significant competitive advantage.

Overall, technology has become an integral part of the modern business landscape, and companies that fail to leverage it effectively are likely to fall behind their competitors. Therefore, businesses must stay abreast of technological developments and adapt their strategies accordingly to remain competitive in the long term.

Competitive Factors

Competitive factors refer to the competitive environment in which a company operates. This includes both direct competitors and potential new entrants to the market. Companies must understand their competi- tors' strengths and weaknesses, as well as their competitive advantages, to develop a business strategy that positions them for success. This may involve differentiating their products or services, entering new markets, or developing new partnerships or collaborations.

It's important to note that the external environment is constantly changing and evolving, and companies must be able to adapt to these changes to stay competitive. This means regularly monitoring and analyzing the external environment to identify potential opportunities and threats, and adjusting the business strategy as needed.

It's important for companies to regularly monitor and analyze the external environment to identify potential opportunities and threats. This may involve conducting market research, attending industry conferences and trade shows, and tracking trends and developments in the industry. By staying up-to-date with the external environment, companies can develop a business strategy that is flexible and adaptable to changing conditions.

4

Setting Goals and Objectives

One of the most critical steps in developing a successful business strategy is setting clear and achievable goals and objectives. Goals and objectives provide a roadmap for the company and help to ensure that everyone in the organization is working towards a common vision. In this chapter, we will discuss the importance of setting goals and objectives and provide some tips for doing so effectively.

1. Importance of Setting Goals and Objectives

   Setting clear and achievable goals and objectives is essential for several reasons. Firstly, goals and objectives help to provide focus and direction for the organization. They allow the company to prioritize its efforts and resources towards achieving specific outcomes. Additionally, goals and objectives help to motivate employees by providing a clear sense of purpose and direction. They can also help to measure progress and success, which is essential for evaluating the effectiveness of the company's strategy.

2. Tips for Setting Effective Goals and Objectives

a) Specific: Goals and objectives should be specific and clearly defined. They should be focused on achieving specific outcomes rather than general aspirations.

b) Measurable: Goals and objectives should be measurable so that progress can be tracked and success can be evaluated.

c) Achievable: Goals and objectives should be realistic and achievable. They should stretch the organization but not be so difficult that they become demotivating.

d) Relevant: Goals and objectives should be relevant to the company's overall strategy and vision. They should align with the company's core competencies and market position.

e) Time-bound: Goals and objectives should be time-bound, with specific deadlines for achieving them. This helps to ensure that the company remains focused and motivated to achieve the desired outcomes.

3. Types of Goals and Objectives
There are several types of goals and objectives that companies may set, depending on their specific circumstances and objectives. These include:

a) Financial Goals: Financial goals are focused on achieving specific financial outcomes, such as revenue growth or profitability.

b) Market Share Goals: Market share goals are focused on increasing the company's market share within its industry.

c) Product Development Goals: Product development goals are focused on developing new products or services or improving existing ones.

d) Operational Efficiency Goals: Operational efficiency goals are focused on improving the efficiency and effectiveness of the company's operations.

e) Employee Development Goals: Employee development goals are focused on developing the skills and capabilities of the company's employees.

4. Cascading Goals and Objectives

Once the company has set its goals and objectives, it is essential to cascade them throughout the organization. This involves communicating the goals and objectives to all employees and ensuring that everyone understands their role in achieving them. It may also involve setting departmental or individual goals that align with the company's overall goals and objectives.

To set effective goals and objectives, it is important to take a comprehensive approach that involves analyzing the company's strengths and weaknesses, assessing the competitive landscape, and understanding market trends and customer needs. This process can help to identify areas where the company can focus its efforts and resources to achieve the greatest impact.

Additionally, when setting goals and objectives, it is important to consider the company's long-term vision and strategic priorities. For example, if the company's long-term goal is to expand into new markets, it may need to set goals and objectives related to market research, product development, and distribution.

Another key aspect of setting effective goals and objectives is to ensure that they are aligned with the company's values and culture. This can help to ensure that employees are motivated and engaged in achieving the desired outcomes.

To ensure that goals and objectives are achievable, it is important to involve key stakeholders in the goal-setting process. This can include employees, customers, suppliers, and other partners. By involving these stakeholders, the company can ensure that its goals and objectives are realistic, relevant, and aligned with the needs of its stakeholders.

Finally, it is important to regularly review and adjust goals and objectives as needed. The business environment is constantly evolving, and goals and objectives that were once relevant and achievable may no longer be so. Regular review and adjustment can help to ensure that the company remains focused on achieving its desired outcomes and adapting to changing circumstances.

In conclusion, setting clear and achievable goals and objectives is essential for developing a successful business strategy. By following the tips outlined in this chapter and considering the different types of goals and objectives, companies can develop a roadmap for success and ensure that everyone in the organization is working towards a common vision.

5

Developing a Business Model

Developing a business model is not a one-time exercise but an ongoing process that requires regular review and adjustment. As a company grows and evolves, its business model may need to be updated to reflect changes in the market or in the company's strategy and objectives.

When developing a business model, it is important to consider the company's strengths and weaknesses, as well as its external environ- ment. This includes understanding the competition, market trends, and customer needs and preferences.

One important aspect of developing a business model is identifying the company's unique value proposition. This refers to the value that the company's product or service offers to customers and should be clear and compelling. A strong value proposition can help to differentiate the company from its competitors and create a competitive advantage. Clients always spend based on the value that the service or product brings to them and thus how pricing is determined, hence why the "Sell me this pen" analogy comes about.

Another key aspect of developing a business model is identifying the target market. This involves understanding the needs and preferences of the customers that the company intends to serve. By understanding the target market, the company can better tailor its product or service to meet customer needs and preferences.

The revenue streams and cost structure are also critical components of the business model. The business model should identify the various ways in which the company plans to generate revenue and should outline the pricing strategy for each. The cost structure should identify the major costs associated with operating the business and outline strategies for reducing or managing those costs. A good rule of thump is 20% of your customer should make 80% of your profit, simply put 20% of your sales should cover your cost of operating the business.

Key partnerships are also an important aspect of the business model. This refers to the relationships that the company needs to build in order to deliver its product or service. The business model should identify the key partners and outline the nature of those partnerships.

A business model is a framework that describes how a company creates, delivers, and captures value. It outlines the way in which a company intends to generate revenue and make a profit. Developing a business model is a critical step in building a successful business, as it helps to define the company's overall strategy and direction.

There are many different types of business models, each with its own strengths and weaknesses. Some common business models include:

1. Product-based business model: This model focuses on creating and selling a product. It involves designing, manufacturing, and distributing products to customers.

2. Service-based business model: This model focuses on providing a service to customers. It involves delivering services that meet customer needs and expectations.

3. Subscription-based business model: This model involves providing a product or service on a recurring basis, typically through a subscription. Examples of subscription-based business models include software as a service (SaaS) and streaming media services.

4. Freemium business model: This model involves providing a basic service or product for free, and then charging customers for premium features or add-ons.

5. Marketplace business model: This model involves creating a platform that connects buyers and sellers. Examples of marketplace business models include eBay and Airbnb.

When developing a business model, it is important to consider several key factors, including:

1. Value proposition: This refers to the unique value that the company's product or service offers to customers. The value proposition should be clear and compelling and should differentiate the company from its competitors.

2. Target market: This refers to the specific group of customers that the company intends to serve. Understanding the needs and preferences of the target market is critical to developing a successful business model.

3. Revenue streams: This refers to the various ways in which the company plans to generate revenue. The business model should identify the primary revenue streams and outline the pricing strat- egy for each. At times this is referred to as lateral extension where the services or products associated with your primary product or service are added on to.

4. Cost structure: This refers to the various costs associated with operating the business. The business model should identify the major costs and outline strategies for reducing or managing those costs.

5. Key partnerships: This refers to the relationships that the company needs to build in order to deliver its product or service. The business model should identify the key partners and outline the nature of those partnerships.

6. Determine your distribution channels: Decide how you will reach your target customers. Will you sell directly to customers or use intermediaries such as distributors or retailers?

Determining your distribution channels is a critical aspect of developing a business model. It refers to the process of deciding how you will deliver your products or services to your target customers. Here are some common distribution channels that businesses use:

- Direct selling: This involves selling products or services directly to customers without any intermediaries. It can be done through a physical store, website, or social media.

- Retail: This involves selling products through retail stores such as department stores, supermarkets, or speciality stores. It is an effective distribution channel for businesses that produce physical goods.

- Wholesaling: This involves selling products in bulk to intermediaries such as retailers or distributors, who then sell the products to end customers.

- Online marketplace: This involves selling products through online marketplaces such as Amazon, Etsy, or eBay. It is an effective distribution channel for businesses that produce physical goods or digital products.

- Direct mail: This involves selling products through direct mail campaigns, such as catalogs or brochures. It is an effective distribution channel for businesses that produce physical goods.
- Partnering with other businesses: This involves partnering with other businesses to distribute your products or services. For exam- ple, a software company may partner with a hardware manufacturer to bundle their products.

When choosing a distribution channel, it is essential to consider factors such as the target customer, product type, and cost-effectiveness. It is also important to continually evaluate and adjust your distribution strategy to ensure that it aligns with your business goals and objectives.

Developing a business model is an iterative process that requires ongoing refinement and adjustment. By taking a comprehensive approach and considering all of the key factors, companies can create a business model that is aligned with their overall strategy and objectives, and that is well-positioned to succeed in the marketplace.

Finally, developing a business model is an iterative process that requires ongoing refinement and adjustment. As the company grows and evolves, its business model may need to be updated to reflect changes in the market or in the company's strategy and objectives. By regularly reviewing and adjusting the business model, companies can ensure they remain well-positioned to succeed in the marketplace.

6

Marketing Strategy

To develop a successful marketing strategy, it is important to understand the market, the competition, and the target customer. This involves conducting market research to identify customer needs, preferences, and behaviours. It is also important to analyze the competition to understand their **strengths** and **weaknesses**, as well as the **opportunities** and **threats** (SWOT) in the market.

Once the target market has been identified, the company should focus on developing a unique value proposition that differentiates it from the competition. This can be achieved by offering high-quality products or services, superior customer service, or unique features that solve customer problems or meet their needs.

The choice of marketing channels is also critical to the success of the marketing strategy. It is important to select channels that are effective in reaching the target customer and that fit within the company's budget and resources. This may involve using a combination of traditional and digital marketing channels, such as advertising, public relations, social media, email marketing, and content marketing.

Setting marketing objectives is an essential component of the marketing strategy. These objectives should be specific and measurable and should align with the overall business goals. It is important to track progress toward these objectives and make adjustments as needed to ensure that the marketing strategy is effective in achieving the desired results.

Developing a realistic budget is also critical to the success of the marketing strategy. This involves identifying the resources that will be required to implement the marketing plan, as well as the expected return on investment. By allocating resources effectively, companies can ensure that their marketing efforts are focused on the activities that are most likely to achieve the desired results.

Marketing strategy is a critical component of any business plan. A well-designed marketing strategy can help a company to reach its target customers and create demand for its products or services. We will discuss the key elements of a marketing strategy and how they can be used to achieve business objectives a bit more in detail.

1. Define the Target Market

   The first step in developing a marketing strategy is to define the target market. This involves identifying the customers that the company intends to serve, as well as their needs and preferences. By understanding the target market, the company can better tailor its marketing efforts to meet customer needs and preferences.

   Conduct market research: Conduct market research to gain insights into your potential customers. This can involve surveys, interviews, focus groups, or analyzing online search data. This research will help you understand the needs, preferences, and behaviours of your potential customers.

Create customer personas: Based on your research, create customer personas that represent your ideal customers. A persona is a fictional character that represents the key characteristics of your target audience. This includes demographic information such as age, gender, education, and income, as well as psychographic information such as values, interests, and motivations.

Identify customer pain points: Identify the problems or challenges that your potential customers are facing. This will help you create a product or service that addresses their specific needs.

Analyze your competition: Analyze your competition to understand their target market and how you can differentiate your product or service. This can involve analyzing their marketing campaigns, website, social media presence, and customer reviews.

Evaluate market size and growth potential: Evaluate the size and growth potential of your target market. This will help you determine the potential revenue and profitability of your business.

2. Develop a Unique Value Proposition

The second step in developing a marketing strategy is to develop a unique value proposition. This refers to the value that the company's product or service offers to customers and should be clear and compelling. A strong value proposition can help to differentiate the company from its competitors and create a competitive advantage.

Identify your target market: Before you can develop a UVP, you need to understand your target market. This involves identifying their needs, wants, and pain points.

Analyze your competitors: Analyze your competitors to understand their strengths and weaknesses. This will help you identify gaps in the market that your product or service can fill.

Define your unique benefits: Define the unique benefits that your product or service provides. This could include features such as quality, convenience, speed, or cost-effectiveness.

Highlight the benefits for your target market: Highlight how your unique benefits will solve the problems or meet the needs of your target market. Use language that resonates with your target market and communicates the value that your product or service provides.

Use a clear and concise statement: Your UVP should be clear, concise, and easy to understand. It should communicate the benefits of your product or service in a way that is compelling and memorable.

Test and refine: Test your UVP with your target market to see how it resonates with them. Use their feedback to refine your UVP and make it more effective.

3. Choose Marketing Channels

The third step in developing a marketing strategy is to choose the marketing channels that will be used to reach the target market. This may include advertising, public relations, social media, email marketing, and other channels. The choice of marketing channels will depend on the target market and the company's budget and resources.

4. Set Marketing Objectives

The fourth step in developing a marketing strategy is to set marketing objectives. These objectives should be specific, measurable, achievable, relevant, and time-bound. Examples of marketing objectives may include increasing website traffic, generating leads, increasing brand awareness, or increasing sales.

5. Develop a Budget

The fifth step in developing a marketing strategy is to develop a budget. This involves identifying the resources that will be required to implement the marketing strategy, as well as the expected return on investment (ROI). The budget should be realistic and should take into account the costs of marketing channels, personnel, and other expenses.

6. Implement the Marketing Strategy

The final step in developing a marketing strategy is to implement the strategy. This involves executing the marketing plan, monitoring progress, and making adjustments as needed. It is important to measure the results of the marketing strategy and adjust the plan as needed to ensure that the company is achieving its marketing objectives.

In summary, developing a marketing strategy is a critical component of any business plan. By defining the target market, developing a unique value proposition, choosing marketing channels, setting marketing objectives, developing a budget, and implementing the marketing strategy, companies can effectively reach their target customers and create demand for their products or services.

Finally, it is important to implement the marketing strategy effectively and monitor progress closely. This involves executing the marketing plan, tracking results, and making adjustments as needed. By continuously analyzing the results of the marketing strategy and making adjustments as needed, companies can ensure that their marketing efforts are effective in achieving their business goals.

7

Sales Strategy

Developing an effective sales strategy is essential for businesses seeking long-term success. A sales strategy involves the approach and methods used to generate revenue and close sales. In this chapter, we will explore the key elements of a successful sales strategy.

In today's competitive business landscape, having a well-developed sales strategy is crucial for the success of any business. A sales strategy is more than just a plan for selling a product or service; it is a comprehensive approach that involves identifying target customers, understanding the sales process, creating sales goals, building a sales team, using technology, establishing sales processes, and measuring sales performance.

One of the most critical aspects of developing a sales strategy is identifying the target customer. This involves creating a detailed profile of the ideal customer, including demographic information such as age, gender, income, and education level, as well as their preferences and behaviours. Understanding the target customer is essential in creating a sales strategy that speaks directly to their needs and interests, and it is crucial for creating effective marketing campaigns and sales pitches.

In addition to identifying the target customer, businesses must also understand the sales process. This includes the various stages of closing a sale, from prospecting to closing the deal. Each stage requires a different approach and set of skills, and it is important to have a clear understanding of each stage to ensure that the sales team is prepared to handle any situation that may arise.

Creating Sales Goals

Sales goals should be specific, measurable, and achievable. They should align with the overall business objectives and provide a clear roadmap for the sales team. Sales goals can be broken down into individual and team objectives to provide a sense of ownership and motivation for the sales team.

In business, a sales team is a group of individuals responsible for selling a company's products or services to customers. The importance of a strong sales team in business cannot be overstated as it is one of the key drivers of revenue growth and profitability.

Building a strong sales team is crucial for the success of any sales strategy. This involves hiring experienced and knowledgeable sales representa- tives who are passionate about the product or service. Providing ongoing training and support is also crucial to ensure that the sales team has the skills and resources they need to succeed.

A strong sales team can help a business achieve its objectives in several ways. Firstly, a strong sales team can help a business to identify new opportunities and potential markets for its products or services. Through their interactions with customers and prospects, sales team members can gather valuable feedback that can help a business to improve its offerings and tailor its marketing efforts to better meet the needs of its target audience.

Secondly, a strong sales team can help a business to increase its revenue by closing more deals and generating more sales. Sales team members are typically skilled negotiators and are able to identify and address the objections and concerns of potential customers. They can also work closely with marketing and product development teams to develop targeted sales strategies that align with the company's overall goals.

A strong sales team can help to build and maintain strong relationships with customers, which is crucial for long-term success. By providing exceptional customer service and support, sales team members can help to build trust and loyalty with customers, which can lead to repeat business and referrals.

Technology can play a critical role in a successful sales strategy. For example, using customer relationship management (CRM) software can help businesses manage customer interactions, track leads, and monitor the sales pipeline. Other technology tools such as email marketing software and social media platforms can also be used to generate leads and close sales. This can help the management to monitor and forecast their revenue and recognize their cash flow for expansion plans.

Understanding the Sales Process

The next step is to understand the sales process, including the stages involved in closing a sale. This includes prospecting, qualifying leads, presenting the product or service, handling objections, and closing the sale. By understanding the sales process, businesses can identify areas for improvement and streamline the sales process to increase efficiency and effectiveness. Establishing clear sales processes is another critical element of a successful sales strategy. This includes creating sales scripts, establishing a consistent follow-up process, and setting clear expectations for the sales team. Regularly reviewing and updating sales processes ensures they remain effective in meeting the needs of the business and the target customer. It's a good practice to have Standard Operating Procedure for every department paired with checklists to ensure a smooth process every time, do take note that an SOP is not cast in stone and is ever evolving to the PEST changes.

Measuring sales performance is a critical aspect of managing a sales team and improving the overall effectiveness of a business. There are several key metrics that can be used to measure sales performance, including:

1. Sales Revenue: This is the total amount of revenue generated by the sales team over a given period of time. Tracking sales revenue is important as it is a clear indicator of how well the team is performing in terms of generating revenue for the business.
2. Sales Volume: Sales volume refers to the total number of products or services sold by the sales team. This metric is useful in understanding the overall sales activity of the team and can help to identify areas where improvements may be needed.
3. Average Deal Size: Average deal size is the average value of each sale made by the sales team. This metric can be useful in identifying trends in customer behaviour and can help to identify opportunities for up-selling and cross-selling.
4. Sales Conversion Rate: The sales conversion rate is the percentage of leads or prospects that convert into paying customers. This metric can be useful in identifying areas where the sales team may need additional training or support.
5. Sales Pipeline: The sales pipeline refers to the number of potential

sales that are currently in progress. This metric can be useful in identifying potential revenue streams and can help to identify areas where the sales team may need additional support or resources.

In addition to these metrics, it is also important to track other factors such as customer satisfaction, sales team morale, and overall business performance. By regularly measuring and analyzing sales performance metrics, businesses can identify areas for improvement, make data-driven decisions, and ultimately achieve their sales and revenue goals.

In conclusion, a successful sales strategy requires a deep understanding of the target customer, the sales process, and the tools and resources needed to close sales. By identifying target customers, creating sales goals, building a sales team, using technology, establishing sales processes, and measuring sales performance, businesses can develop a sales strategy that is effective in generating revenue and achieving long- term success. A well-developed sales strategy is essential for the long- term success of any business. By understanding the target customer, the sales process, and the tools and resources needed to close sales, businesses can create a sales strategy that is effective in generating revenue and achieving business objectives.

8

Financial Planning and Management

One of the most critical aspects of running a successful business is financial planning and management. This involves understanding your company's financial situation and developing strategies to ensure that your business remains financially stable and profitable in the long term. In this chapter, we will discuss the key components of financial planning and management, including budgeting, forecasting, cash flow management, and financial analysis.

Financial Goals

Financial goals are the specific targets or objectives that a business aims to achieve in terms of its financial performance. These goals typically relate to the amount of revenue, profits, or cash flow business plans generate within a given period, as well as the level of financial stability and solvency it aims to maintain. Some common financial goals that businesses may set for themselves include:

1. Increasing revenue: This may involve setting targets for sales growth, increasing market share, or expanding into new markets or product lines.

2. Maximizing profits: Businesses may set goals for increasing profit margins or reducing costs to improve their bottom line.
3. Generating cash flow: This may involve setting targets for increasing cash reserves, improving cash flow management, or reducing debt.
4. Achieving financial stability: Businesses may aim to maintain a certain level of financial stability, such as maintaining a healthy debt-to-equity ratio or maintaining a certain level of cash reserves.
5. Investing in growth: Businesses may set financial goals around investing in growth opportunities, such as expanding facilities or launching new products, to achieve long-term growth and success

Budgeting

Budgeting involves creating a detailed financial plan for a specific period, such as a month, quarter, or year. To create an effective budget, you should first identify all sources of income and all expenses. This could include revenue from sales, investments, or loans, and expenses such as rent, payroll, inventory, and marketing expenses.

Once you have identified your sources of income and expenses, you can create a budget that balances them and helps you achieve your financial goals. The budget should be realistic and achievable, based on your historical financial data and any projections or assumptions about future revenue and expenses.

Budgeting is the process of creating a financial plan for your business, which outlines your projected income and expenses for a specific period. Creating a budget allows you to forecast your financial situation and plan your expenditures accordingly. To create an effective budget, you should consider your company's historical financial data, sales projections, and any upcoming investments or expenses. Once you have developed your budget, it is essential to monitor and update it regularly to ensure that you remain on track.

Regularly monitoring your budget is essential to ensure that you are on track to achieve your financial goals. You should regularly compare your actual revenue and expenses to your budgeted amounts and make adjustments as needed to ensure that you remain on track.

Forecasting

Forecasting finance in business involves estimating the financial outcomes of a business over a specific period, typically the next fiscal year. This process can be crucial for planning, budgeting, and decision-making purposes. Here are some steps to follow to forecast finance in business:

1. Gather historical financial data: Collect and analyze the business's financial statements from the previous years, including balance sheets, income statements, and cash flow statements.
2. Identify trends and patterns: Look for trends and patterns in the historical financial data that can be used to make assumptions about future performance.
3. Determine key assumptions: Based on the trends and patterns identified, determine key assumptions about future financial performance. This may include assumptions about sales growth, operating expenses, capital expenditures, and other factors that impact financial performance.
4. Develop financial projections: Using the historical data and assumptions, develop financial projections for the next fiscal year, including projected revenue, expenses, profits, and cash flow.

5. Review and adjust projections: Review the financial projections to ensure they are reasonable and achievable. Adjust the projections as needed based on changes in the business environment or new information.

6. Monitor and update projections: Monitor actual financial performance throughout the year and update the financial projections as necessary to reflect any changes in business conditions or assumptions.

Forecasting involves predicting future financial performance based on historical data and market trends. To effectively forecast your financial performance, you need to have access to accurate data and a solid understanding of the market and industry trends. Forecasting helps you anticipate potential challenges or opportunities and develop strategies to address them proactively. For example, if your forecasting shows that your revenue is likely to decline in the upcoming quarter, you can develop a plan to cut expenses or increase marketing efforts to offset the decline.

It's important to note that forecasting finance in business is not an exact science, and there are many variables that can impact financial performance. However, by following these steps and regularly monitoring and updating financial projections, businesses can improve their ability to plan, budget, and make informed decisions.

Cash Flow Management

Managing cash flow is crucial for the success of any business, regardless of size or industry. Here are some steps to follow to effectively manage cash flow in business:

1. Create a cash flow projection: Develop a projection of your cash inflows and outflows for the next 12 months. This will help you anticipate cash shortages and surpluses and make informed decisions.

2. Manage accounts receivable: Invoice promptly and follow up on overdue payments. Offer incentives for early payment, and consider implementing a credit policy to manage risk.

3. Control inventory: Keep inventory levels in check to avoid over-stocking and tying up cash. Monitor inventory turnover and identify slow-moving items that may need to be discounted or liquidated.

4. Manage accounts payable: Negotiate favourable payment terms with suppliers, and take advantage of early payment discounts. Pay bills on time to avoid late fees and penalties.

5. Monitor cash flow regularly: Review your cash flow projection regularly and compare it to actual results. Identify any variances and take corrective action if necessary.

6. Control expenses: Monitor your expenses carefully and look for opportunities to reduce costs. Consider outsourcing non-core functions or renegotiating contracts to save money.

7. Consider financing options: Evaluate financing options such as lines of credit, loans, or factoring to help manage cash flow during periods of tight cash.

Cash flow management involves monitoring and managing the inflow and outflow of cash in your business. Managing your cash flow effectively requires you to maintain a positive cash flow, manage accounts payable and accounts receivable, and have sufficient reserves to cover unexpected expenses.

To manage your cash flow effectively, you should regularly monitor your cash flow statement, which shows the cash inflows and outflows of your business over a specific period. This allows you to identify potential cash flow issues and take action to address them proactively.

Managing your accounts payable and accounts receivable is also critical to maintaining a healthy cash flow. This involves monitoring your invoices and payments and following up with customers or vendors as needed to ensure timely payments.

Financial Analysis

Financial analysis involves reviewing your company's financial data to identify trends, strengths, and weaknesses. This allows you to make informed decisions about investments, expenses, and other financial decisions.

To conduct effective financial analysis, you need to have access to accurate and up-to-date financial data. You should regularly review your income statement, balance sheet, and cash flow statement to identify trends and make informed decisions about your financial situation.

Financial analysis can help you identify areas where you may be overspending or missing opportunities for revenue growth. By analyzing your financial data regularly, you can make informed decisions to improve your financial performance and achieve long-term success.

Here are some steps to follow to conduct financial analysis in business:

1. Collect financial data: Gather financial statements such as income statements, balance sheets, and cash flow statements. Additionally, collect other relevant financial data such as sales figures, inventory levels, and accounts receivable aging reports.

2. Calculate financial ratios: Use financial ratios to analyze the business's financial performance. Common ratios include profitability ratios such as gross profit margin, net profit margin, and return on assets; liquidity ratios such as current ratio and quick ratio; and

   solvency ratios such as debt-to-equity ratio and interest coverage ratio.

3. Compare ratios to industry benchmarks: Compare the business's financial ratios to industry benchmarks to evaluate its financial performance relative to competitors.

4. Analyze trends: Analyze trends in financial data over time to identify patterns or changes in the business's financial performance. This may include changes in sales, margins, expenses, or other financial metrics.

5. Conduct a SWOT analysis: Conduct a SWOT analysis (strengths, weaknesses, opportunities, and threats) to evaluate the business's financial position in relation to its competition and the broader market.

6. Interpret findings: Interpret the financial analysis findings to identify strengths and weaknesses in the business's financial performance. Use this information to make strategic decisions about the business's future direction and to identify areas for improvement.

Overall, financial analysis provides valuable insights into a business's financial performance and helps business owners and managers make informed decisions about the future of their business.

9

Operations Strategy

Operations strategy involves the development of a plan to effectively manage the resources, processes, and activities required to produce and deliver a product or service. This includes manufacturing, supply chain management, inventory management, and quality control.

To develop an effective operations strategy, you should consider the following key components:

1. Capacity Planning: Capacity planning involves determining the resources needed to produce a certain level of output. This includes identifying the equipment, labour, and other resources needed to produce and deliver your product or service. Capacity planning can help you optimize production efficiency, reduce waste, and ensure that you can meet customer demand.

2. Supply Chain Management: Supply chain management involves managing the flow of goods and services from suppliers to customers. This includes identifying reliable suppliers, managing inventory levels, and developing efficient transportation and delivery systems. Effective supply chain management can help you

reduce costs, improve quality, and enhance customer satisfaction.

3. Inventory Management: Inventory management involves managing the amount of inventory you have on hand to ensure that you can meet customer demand while minimizing waste and excess inventory. Effective inventory management requires a balance between maintaining adequate stock levels and avoiding overstocking, which can tie up valuable resources. In today's day and age, most companies have gone into Lean Logistics which will be explained further below.

4. Quality Control: Quality control involves ensuring that your product or service meets the established quality standards. This includes developing quality control processes and procedures, training employees, and regularly monitoring and analyzing performance data. Effective quality control can help you build customer loyalty and reputation while minimizing the risk of product recalls or other quality-related issues. The best way to increase profits is to reduce resource wastage this is also true for Service orientate operations where the wastage is the manhours that are utilized for the job.

5. Process Improvement: Process improvement involves analyzing your operational processes and identifying opportunities for improvement. This could involve implementing lean manufacturing principles, using technology to automate processes, or developing more efficient workflows. By continuously improving your operational processes, you can increase efficiency, reduce costs, and improve quality.

6. Risk Management: Risk management involves identifying potential risks to your business operations and developing strategies to

mitigate those risks. This could include developing contingency plans for supply chain disruptions, implementing safety protocols to protect employees, or developing business continuity plans to address unexpected events. This is why SWOT and PEST strategies are considered at frequent intervals of the company strategies especially when there are new services, products or changes in company structure.

By developing an effective operations strategy, you can optimize your production and delivery processes, reduce costs, and enhance the quality of your products or services. This can help you build a competitive advantage and achieve long-term success in your industry.

* * *

In addition to the key components mentioned above, there are other factors to consider when developing an effective operations strategy. These include:

1. Sustainability: Sustainability involves considering the environmental, social, and economic impacts of your business operations. This includes reducing waste, minimizing energy consumption, and implementing sustainable sourcing practices. By prioritizing sustainability, you can reduce your environmental footprint and enhance your reputation among customers and stakeholders.

2. Technology: Technology plays a critical role in modern business operations. By leveraging technology, you can improve productivity, enhance data analysis, and automate repetitive tasks. This could include implementing inventory management software, using data analytics tools to monitor performance, or investing in

automated manufacturing equipment.

3. Outsourcing: Outsourcing involves contracting with external suppliers or service providers to perform certain business functions. This could include outsourcing manufacturing, distribution, or customer service functions. Outsourcing can help you reduce costs and enhance operational efficiency, but it also introduces risks such as quality control issues or supply chain disruptions. Outsourcing is also associated with startups a lot due to the fact that there are service providers and suppliers who do the larger quantity of the job required and can provide the service or product at a cheaper cost compared to a startup company doing lower quantities. A good rule of thump is to invest in equipment or manpower only once the demand and jobs make profitable sense when scaling one's operations.

4. Continuous Improvement: Continuous improvement involves implementing a culture of ongoing improvement and innovation. This could involve encouraging employee feedback, implementing employee training programs, or regularly monitoring and analyzing performance metrics. By continuously improving your operations, you can stay ahead of competitors and adapt to changing market conditions.

5. Customer Focus: Your operations strategy should be designed with a focus on meeting the needs and expectations of your customers. This involves understanding their preferences and priorities and developing processes that prioritize customer satisfaction. By putting your customers first, you can build a loyal customer base and enhance your reputation. Hence, keeping an eye on the market changes and being flexible enough to change is important for the

survivability of any organization.

Lean Logistics

Lean logistics is an approach to logistics and supply chain management that focuses on minimizing waste, maximizing efficiency, and creating value for customers. It draws its principles from the lean manufacturing philosophy pioneered by Toyota, which aims to eliminate non-value- added activities and optimize the flow of materials, information, and resources.

In lean logistics, the emphasis is placed on reducing various forms of waste, such as excess inventory, overproduction, transportation inefficiencies, waiting times, and defects. The goal is to create a streamlined and agile supply chain that delivers products or services to customers in the most efficient and cost-effective manner possible.

Some key principles and practices associated with lean logistics include:

1. Just-in-Time (JIT) Delivery: JIT involves delivering materials or components to the production line or customer's location at the precise time they are needed, minimizing inventory holding costs and reducing waste.

2. Continuous Improvement: Lean logistics promotes a culture of continuous improvement, where employees at all levels of the organization are encouraged to identify and eliminate waste, streamline processes, and make incremental improvements over time.

3. Value Stream Mapping: Value stream mapping is a technique used to identify and analyze the flow of materials, information, and processes involved in delivering a product or service. It helps identify areas of waste and opportunities for improvement.

4. Kanban System: The Kanban system is a visual signalling method that helps manage inventory levels and production flow. It uses

cards or other visual cues to signal the need for replenishment or production of a specific item.

5. Cross-Functional Collaboration: Lean logistics encourages collaboration and communication among different departments and stakeholders involved in the supply chain. This collaboration helps identify bottlenecks, improve coordination, and reduce waste across the entire value chain.

6. Total Quality Management (TQM): Lean logistics emphasizes the importance of quality in all aspects of the supply chain. By focusing on quality control and continuous improvement, organizations can reduce defects, rework, and customer complaints.

By implementing lean logistics principles, organizations can achieve benefits such as improved operational efficiency, reduced costs, shorter lead times, increased customer satisfaction, and a more responsive and adaptable supply chain.

Overall, an effective operations strategy requires a holistic approach that considers a range of factors, including capacity planning, supply chain management, inventory management, quality control, sustainability, technology, outsourcing, continuous improvement, and customer focus. By developing a comprehensive strategy that addresses all of these factors, you can optimize your operations and achieve long-term success in your industry.

10

Human Resource Strategy

The success of any business depends on its people. An effective human resource strategy is essential for attracting, developing, and retaining top talent. In this chapter, we will explore the key components of a successful human resource strategy.

1. An effective recruitment and selection process involves identifying the skills and qualities required for a particular role, developing job descriptions and advertisements, and using a range of recruitment methods to attract the best candidates. Some of the recruitment methods that businesses can use include job boards, social media platforms, employee referrals, and professional networking sites. An effective recruitment and selection process should be efficient, streamlined, and objective, with clear evaluation criteria, used to assess candidates' suitability for the role. It is also essential to ensure that the process is fair and inclusive, with efforts made to eliminate bias and discrimination. Always consider fair employment practices such as Singapore's TAFEP guidelines.

2. Employee development is critical for enhancing employee

performance, improving employee retention, and building a culture of continuous learning. Some of the employee development initiatives that businesses can use include providing on-the-job training, offering professional development opportunities, or providing mentoring or coaching programs. An effective employee development program should be aligned with the organization's goals and objectives, and tailored to meet the needs of individual employees. By providing employees with opportunities to learn and grow, businesses can enhance employee engagement, improve retention rates, and develop a skilled and motivated workforce. Many organisations find it difficult to spare the manpower and operations time required for training their manpower however it is a vital ingredient to the professional effective execution of the company's job roles.

3. Performance management: Performance management involves setting clear expectations for employee performance, providing regular feedback, and monitoring progress towards goals. An effective performance management system should be based on clear performance metrics and should involve regular performance reviews and goal setting. It is essential to ensure that the performance metrics used are relevant to the role and the organization's goals and objectives. Regular feedback is also critical, as it provides employees with a clear understanding of how they are performing, areas where they need to improve, and opportunities for recognition and rewards. The Performance matrix is a subset derived from the company's KPIs.

4. Compensation and benefits: Compensation and benefits are critical components of any human resource strategy. An effective compensation and benefits strategy should be competitive, fair,

and aligned with the organization's goals and values. The compensation package offered should be designed to attract and retain top talent, while also motivating employees to perform at their best. It is essential to ensure that the compensation package is fair and equitable, with efforts made to eliminate any gender or other forms of bias. Benefits such as health insurance, retirement plans, and vacation time can also play a significant role in employee satisfaction and retention. Many startups fall into the trap of overpaying their employees initially and this could lead to employees not working to their full potential which in turn increased the required manpower to complete the same task. Structure-based behavioural science states that adequate compensation with the right motivational benefits is a juggling act that needs to be gotten right early on for effective human resource management.

5. Employee engagement is critical for driving productivity, creativity, and innovation. An engaged workforce is more likely to be motivated, committed, and productive, which can have a significant impact on a business's success. An effective employee engagement strategy should involve regular communication, opportunities for employee feedback, and recognition and rewards for good performance. It is also essential to ensure that employees feel valued, respected, and supported in their roles. By fostering a positive and engaging work environment, businesses can enhance employee satisfaction, reduce turnover rates, and improve overall performance.

For new Entrepreneurs, they tend to do all the tasks themself before they hand them over to the right qualified employee, as this method is not wrong this just makes the entrepreneurs highly paid managers.

The Task of the entrepreneur is to strategies the improvement of the organisation and not be bogged down with day-to-day operations. A famous saying goes that a good entrepreneur is one who is incompetent because an incompetent person will look for the right person to do the job for him/her instead of getting down to do it themself. Keep in mind as an entrepreneur your time is more valuable than the employees which is why hiring the right people to do the tasks for you makes you available to do the more important parts of the business such as expansion and planning.

In Singapore, several organisations with the assistance of the government have come up with Skills Future initiatives where important Sectors for the nation are planned out meticulously and work has a great guide on the required technical skills and core competencies needed for each role in that particular sector and they also propose training needed and provide government support for such courses. Even though you might not be based in Singapore the Career map and skills required is mostly through for most industries around the globe.

In today's time where there are several avenues available for people to make money from the comfort of their homes such as being a social media influencer, motivating employees and retention becomes a challenge. Every individual is a human being who has dreams and is motivated by different things, some are just prisoners of circumstance. It's vital for an employer to recognise the motivational track of the person during the interview process so as hire the right candidate.

Additionally, it's vital to identify the Performance vs Loyalty require- ments for the individual position. Everyone wants a High Performance – High Loyalty Employee but this is ideal and difficult to achieve and may take time. Many organisation during the interview only looks for performance and disregard the loyalty element and ending up having retention problems in the company. A mid-level performer with good loyalty (subject to motivational requirements) is far more appropriate to an organization than a high-performance low-loyalty person. A Low loyal employee can become a virus to the organisation and may take a lot of resources to rectify. A good rule of thumb is performance can be thought and cultivated provided the individual has the right character but loyalty is mostly an inbred personality that needs time to be proven. Even a high loyalty person can lose their loyalty to the organisation   if their requirements are not met hence where the previously stated motivational track identification becomes crucial. In such a fast-paced environment these days there can be many distractions for employees hence a qualified human resource manager or outsourced employment agency's role is to constantly monitor the employee's behaviour to correct it from time to time.

Overall, a comprehensive human resource strategy that includes recruitment and selection, employee development, performance management, compensation and benefits, and employee engagement is critical for achieving long-term business success. By investing in their employees and creating a positive and engaging work environment, businesses can attract and retain top talent, enhance employee performance, and achieve their goals.

11

Risk Management

Introduction: Risk is an inherent part of any business operation, and as such, effective risk management is essential to ensure long-term sustainability and success. Risk management involves identifying, assessing, and mitigating risks that may impact the business's ability to achieve its objectives. In this chapter, we will discuss the importance of risk management, the different types of risks that businesses face, and strategies for mitigating these risks.

A business in simple terms is a process or product that solves a problem, thus problem-solving is what people pay the business for and problems always come with risk managing that risk effectively, efficiently and taking calculated risks is the core of any business.

"A Customer is the most important visitor on our premises. He is not dependent on us. We are dependent on him. He is not an interruption in our work. He is the purpose of it. He is not an outsider in our business. He is part of it. We are not doing him a favour by serving him. He is doing us a favour by giving us an opportunity to do so." ~ Mahatma Gandhi

The Importance of Risk Management: Effective risk management is critical for any business operation as it helps to reduce uncertainty and increase the likelihood of achieving business objectives. By identifying potential risks and developing strategies to manage them, businesses can protect themselves from unexpected events that may result in financial losses, reputational damage, or legal liability.

Types of Business Risks: There are various types of risks that businesses face, including:

1. Strategic Risks: These are risks that arise from business strategy decisions, such as entering into a new market or developing a new product.

   Strategic risks can manifest in various forms. For instance, disruptive technologies can render existing business models obsolete, posing a risk to organizations that fail to adapt. Changes in regulations or government policies can create uncertainties and impact an organization's strategic initiatives. Shifts in consumer preferences and market trends can erode market share and competitive advantage. Poorly executed mergers or acquisitions can result in financial losses and operational inefficiencies.

2. Financial Risks:

   Financial risks refer to the potential threats or uncertainties that can adversely affect the financial health, stability, and performance of an individual, organization, or investment. These risks can arise from various sources, including market volatility, economic conditions, creditworthiness, liquidity, interest rates, currency fluctuations, and regulatory changes. Effectively managing financial risks is crucial for maintaining financial stability and achieving long-term financial objectives. Here are some key points to elaborate on financial risks:

Market Risk: Market risk refers to the potential losses arising from changes in market prices, such as stocks, bonds, commodities, or currencies. It encompasses three main types of risk: equity risk, interest rate risk, and commodity risk. Market risk arises due to factors like economic conditions, geopolitical events, investor sentiment, and supply-demand dynamics. Organizations and investors can mitigate market risk through diversification, hedging strategies, and setting risk tolerance limits.

b) Credit Risk: Credit risk arises from the potential failure of a borrower to meet their financial obligations. It can occur in lending activities, trade credit, or investment in debt securities. The creditworthiness of borrowers or counterparties, including individuals, businesses, or governments, can impact the risk of default. Organizations and financial institutions manage credit risk by conducting thorough credit assessments, setting credit limits, implementing risk-based pricing, and establishing credit risk management frameworks. A business should be a good oil machine that multiplies the investment placed into it, as such money borrowed or invested should be considered on the interest percentage. Many companies during difficult times borrow money to keep operations alive and fall into a downward spiral of loans and end up in a business closure hence always consider the purpose of the loan taken or money invested into a business. Fixing the money leakage should be the primary task in such scenarios.

"Spraying perfume does not remove the odour of dead rat in the house it simply just masks the odour temporarily" ~ Karls Karthikeyan

c) Liquidity Risk: Liquidity risk refers to the inability to meet financial obligations or execute transactions in a timely manner due to insufficient available funds or marketability of assets. It can occur when there is a lack of buyers or sellers in a market, unexpected cash outflows, or restricted access to funding sources. Organizations mitigate liquidity risk by maintaining adequate cash reserves, establishing lines of credit, diversifying funding sources, and conducting stress testing to assess liquidity needs. This is why all experts advise that a business should have at least 6 months' worth of savings to run a business to cater for rainy days.

d) Operational Risk: Operational risk arises from inadequate or failed internal processes, systems, people, or external events that can lead to financial losses. It includes risks associated with errors, fraud, technology failures, supply chain disruptions, legal and regulatory compliance, and business continuity. Effective risk management practices, internal controls, employee training, and contingency planning can help mitigate operational risks. This is where business continuity plans play a crucial role, technological disruptions are common these days which is why most data are stored in cloud servers and staff are facilitated and equipped to work from home, of course, this will not apply to all scenarios such as manufacturing, even in such cases companies have part-time staff recallable within the hour, standby generators and machines on standby.

e) Foreign Exchange Risk: Foreign exchange risk, also known as currency risk, arises from fluctuations in exchange rates between currencies. It can impact organizations engaged in international trade, foreign investments, or multinational operations. Changes in exchange rates can affect the value of assets, liabilities, cash flows, and profitability. Organizations manage foreign exchange risk through hedging strategies, such as currency derivatives, or natural hedging by matching revenues and expenses in the same currency. A good method again falls onto the Cash reserves to keep foreign currency long enough to be exchanged at a profitable rate at a later time. Startups that depend on month-to-month cash flow are at the biggest risk of such Foreign Exchange Risks.

f) Regulatory and Compliance Risk: Regulatory and compliance risk refers to the potential financial and reputational harm arising from non-compliance with laws, regulations, and industry standards. It can result in fines, penalties, litigation, damage to reputation, and restrictions on business operations. Organizations mitigate regulatory and compliance risks by establishing robust compliance programs, staying updated on legal and regulatory changes, conducting internal audits, and implementing effective governance and risk management frameworks.

g) Interest Rate Risk: Interest rate risk arises from fluctuations in interest rates, which can affect the cost of borrowing, investment returns, and the value of fixed-income securities. Rising interest rates can increase borrowing costs, reduce bond prices, and impact profitability. Organizations and investors manage interest rate risk through interest rate swaps, options, and other hedging instruments.

3. Reputational Risks: Reputational risk refers to the potential harm to an individual, organization, or brand's reputation resulting from negative public perception, loss of trust, or damage to the

overall image and standing in the eyes of stakeholders, including customers, employees, investors, regulators, and the general public. It can arise from various sources, including unethical behaviour, poor product quality, data breaches, environmental negligence, public scandals, customer complaints, or negative media coverage. Effectively managing reputational risk is essential for maintaining trust, credibility, and long-term success. Here are some key points to elaborate on reputational risk:

a. Importance of Reputation: Reputation is an intangible yet valuable asset that can influence consumer behaviour, investor confidence, employee morale, and business relationships. A strong reputation can enhance customer loyalty, attract investment, and differentiate an organization from its competitors. Conversely, a damaged reputation can lead to customer attrition, investor scepticism, difficulty attracting talent, and financial losses.

b. Impact on Stakeholders: Reputational risk affects a wide range of stakeholders. Customers may lose trust in a brand and switch to competitors, resulting in declining sales and market share. Investors may perceive higher risk and divest from the organization, leading to a drop in stock prices. Employees may become demotivated or seek employment elsewhere, affecting productivity and talent retention. Suppliers and business partners may reconsider their relationships, impacting the organization's ability to operate effectively. Regulators may impose fines or additional compliance requirements due to reputational damage.

c. Sources of Reputational Risk: Reputational risk can emerge from various sources. It may arise from organizational actions or failures, such as product recalls, ethical breaches, financial misconduct, or data breaches. It can also stem from external events, such as negative media coverage, social media backlash, or public controversies related to industry practices. Reputational risk can be intensified by the speed and reach of information dissemination in the digital age.

Risk Mitigation Strategies: There are various strategies that businesses can use to mitigate risks, including:

1. Risk Avoidance: This involves avoiding activities that may expose the business to risk, such as avoiding high-risk investments or exiting a market that is deemed too risky.
2. Risk Reduction: This involves reducing the likelihood or impact of risks, such as implementing safety procedures or diversifying the customer base.
3. Risk Transfer: This involves transferring the risk to another party, such as through insurance policies or outsourcing.
4. Risk Acceptance: This involves accepting the risk and developing contingency plans to manage the potential consequences, such as creating a crisis management plan.
5. Risk Sharing: This involves sharing the risk with other parties, such as joint ventures or partnerships.

Managing Risk:

Identify risks: Start by identifying all potential risks that could affect your business, including financial, operational, legal, and reputational risks. Conduct a risk assessment to determine the likelihood and potential impact of each risk.

1. Assess risks: After identifying potential risks, assess each risk to determine the level of threat it poses to your business. Consider the likelihood of the risk occurring, as well as the potential impact it could have on your business.

2. Develop risk management strategies: Once you have identified and assessed potential risks, develop strategies to mitigate or avoid them. This may involve implementing safeguards, creating contin- gency plans, or transferring risk through insurance or contracts.

3. Monitor and review risks: Risks can change over time, so it's important to continually monitor and review them. Regularly assess the effectiveness of your risk management strategies and adjust them as necessary.

4. Foster a culture of risk management: Finally, it's important to foster a culture of risk management throughout your organization. Encourage employees to identify and report potential risks, and provide training and resources to help them understand how to manage risks effectively.

5. Keep up-to-date with industry standards: Staying up-to-date with industry standards and regulations is essential to managing risk effectively. Be sure to regularly review industry publications, attend relevant conferences or seminars, and seek the advice of experts when necessary.

6. Have a crisis management plan: A crisis management plan is an essential component of effective risk management. Develop a plan that outlines how your organization will respond in the event of a crisis, including procedures for communicating with stakeholders, mobilizing resources, and managing the crisis.

7. Conduct regular risk assessments: Regular risk assessments are critical to identifying new risks and ensuring that existing risks are being effectively managed. Conducting regular assessments also helps ensure that risk management strategies are up-to-date and

aligned with current business objectives.

8. Utilize technology: Technology can play a significant role in managing risk. Consider implementing risk management software or other tools to help automate the risk management process, track and monitor risks, and generate reports and analytics to support decision-making.

9. Monitor and evaluate performance: To ensure that your risk management strategies are effective, it's important to regularly monitor and evaluate their performance. This may involve tracking key performance indicators (KPIs) or conducting periodic audits to ensure compliance with risk management policies and procedures.

The Airline industry has Zero Tolerance for Risks as it has many lives onboard an aircraft thus the systems like Dirty Dozen use constant training and reminders to the staff to identify risk as a collective organisation and making it everyone's responsibility is a good practice to follow.

Conclusion: Effective risk management is an essential component of any business strategy. By identifying potential risks and developing strategies to mitigate them, businesses can protect themselves from un-expected events that may impact their ability to achieve their objectives. It is important for businesses to continually assess and update their risk management strategies to ensure they are effectively managing risks as they arise.

12

Implementation and Evaluation

Implementation and evaluation are critical components of any successful business strategy. While it's important to develop a well-defined strategy, it's equally important to ensure that the strategy is implemented effectively and that its success is regularly evaluated.

When implementing a business strategy, it's important to have a clear plan of action. This plan should include a timeline with specific deadlines for each stage of the implementation process. It's also important to assign responsibilities and allocate resources to ensure that everyone involved in the implementation process knows what is expected of them and has the resources they need to carry out their tasks.

Once a business strategy has been developed, it is essential to implement it effectively and evaluate its effectiveness. This chapter will cover the key aspects of implementing and evaluating a business strategy.

Implementation a business strategy requires a clear plan of action. The following steps should be taken to ensure successful implementation:

- Create a timeline: Set a timeline with specific deadlines for each stage of the implementation process. This will help to ensure that progress is being made and that everyone is on the same page.

- Assign responsibilities: Clearly define the roles and responsibilities of each team member involved in the implementation process. This will help to ensure that everyone knows what is expected of them and that tasks are completed on time.
- Allocate resources: Ensure that the necessary resources, including financial, technological, and human resources, are allocated to support the implementation process.
- Monitor progress: Regularly monitor the progress of the implementation process to ensure that it is on track and that any issues are identified and addressed promptly.

Monitoring progress during the implementation process is crucial to ensuring that everything stays on track. Regular progress reports can help identify any potential issues and address them promptly. In addition, setting up a system for feedback and communication can help ensure that everyone involved in the implementation process is on the same page and can make any necessary adjustments as needed.

Evaluation is equally important in ensuring the success of a business strategy. This involves defining success metrics that align with the overall goals and objectives of the business. Metrics may include financial data, customer feedback, employee feedback, and market data, among others. The following steps should be taken to evaluate the success of a business strategy:

- Define success metrics: Clearly define the metrics that will be used to measure the success of the strategy. These should be aligned with the overall goals and objectives of the business.
- Collect data: Collect relevant data to measure the success metrics.

This may include financial data, customer feedback, employee feedback, and market data.

- Analyze data: Analyze the data collected to determine whether the strategy is achieving the desired outcomes. This will help to identify any areas where changes may be necessary.
- Make adjustments: Based on the analysis, make any necessary adjustments to the strategy to improve its effectiveness.
- Monitor progress: Regularly monitor progress against the success metrics to ensure that the strategy continues to achieve the desired outcomes.

Once the data is collected, it must be analyzed to determine whether the strategy is achieving the desired outcomes. This analysis can help identify areas where changes may be necessary to improve effectiveness. Based on the analysis, adjustments can be made to the strategy, and progress can continue to be monitored to ensure continued success.

In conclusion, implementing and evaluating a business strategy requires careful planning, clear communication, and regular monitoring. By following the steps outlined in this chapter, businesses can ensure that their strategies are effectively implemented and evaluated for success. This will help to identify areas for improvement and ensure continued growth and success.